DATE DUE

NOV 4 '89			
OCT 18			
NOV 26 '90			
MAR 6 '91			
APR 19 '91			
MAY 14 '91			
NOV 6 '91			
MAR 13 '92			
OCT 7 '92			
JAN 19 '93			
FEB 25 '93			
APR 1 '93			
MAY 19 '93			
NOV 3 1993			
JAN 5 1994			
APR 08 1994			
MAY 18 1994			

The Library Store   #47-0103

D1087439

A65500 198030

LOOK AT
EYES

Copyright © 1988 Franklin Watts

First published in the USA by

Franklin Watts Inc
387 Park Avenue South ·
New York 10016

ISBN: 0−531−10549−0
Library of Congress
Catalog Card No: 87−51710

Design: David Bennett
Illustrations: Simon Roulstone

The author and publisher would like
to thank the following for their
participation in the photography
for this book:
Chloe Orford, Duncan Smith, Aruna
Mumtaz, Haruko Takeuchi, Richard
Bernstein, Steven Vischer, Tom Adeney,
Yousuf Khan, Charlie Walker-Wise,
Juliet Atkin, Chloe Andricopoulos,
Leo Thomson (all pupils at the King
Alfred School, London), Kate Tatum,
Alexandra Cragg, Nicola Hickman-
Robertson, Sam London, Chloe Thomson,
Ezra, Zachary and Solveig Emerson.

Optical equipment supplied courtesy of
Broadhurst, Clarkson and Fuller

Additional Photographs
Chris Fairclough p13
Zefa p9, 12, 13, 20, 21, 28

Printed in Italy
by G. Canale & C. S.p.A. Turin

91689

LOOK AT
EYES

Ruth Thomson

Photography by Mike Galletly

FRANKLIN WATTS
London · New York · Sydney · Toronto

Look at eyes.

Eyes are all sorts of colors and shapes.

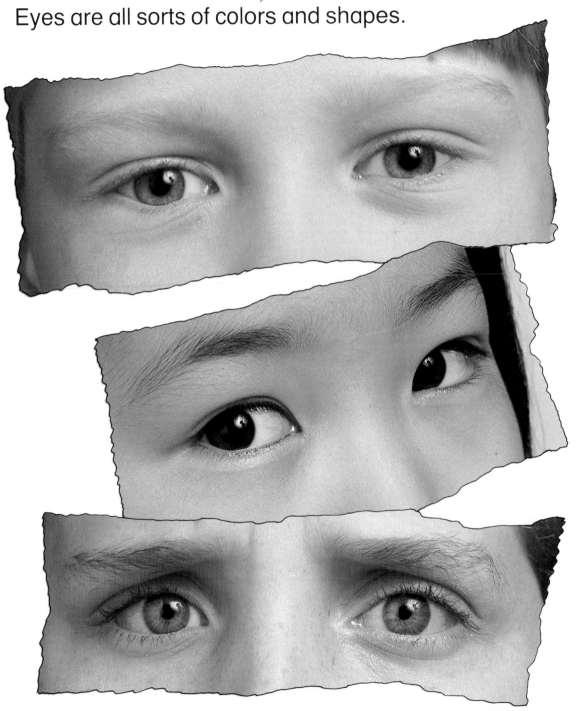

611.84
Tho
copy 1

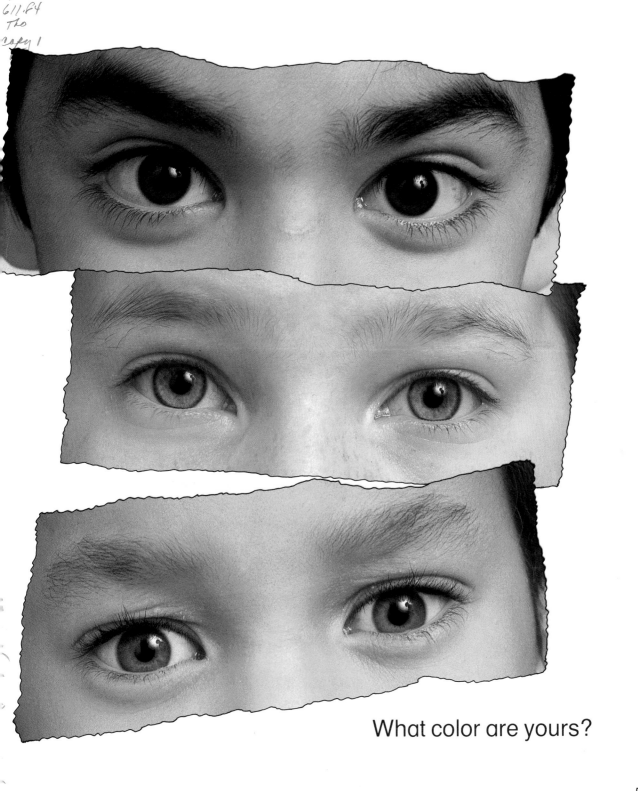

What color are yours?

Eyes are very precious.
You use them every moment that you are awake.

Think of all the things it would be difficult to do
if you couldn't see to do them.

How would you ...

draw or paint?

read or write?

play board games?

throw and catch?

Eyes are well protected.
Gently feel the hard bone
underneath your eyebrow
and all around your eye.
This is the eye socket.
Your eye is set within it.

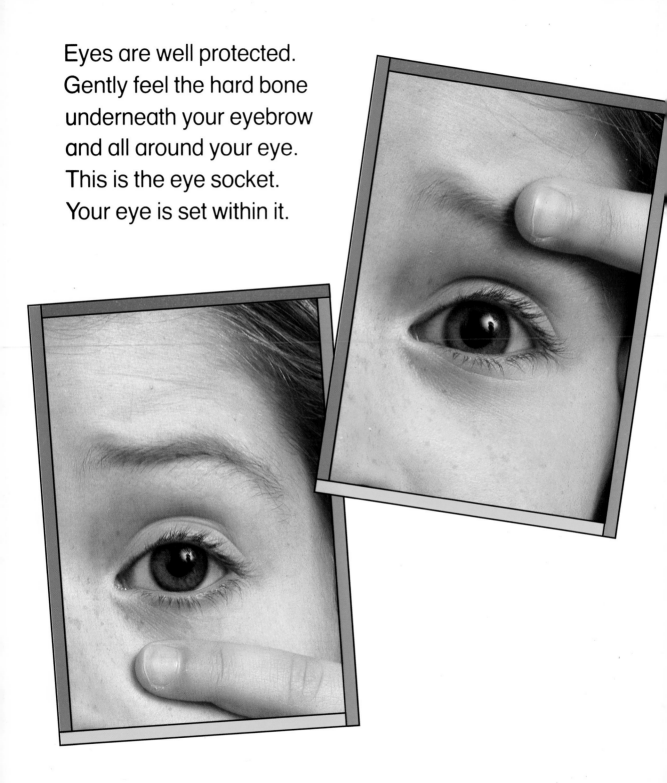

Eyes are shaped like balls.
You can only see a tiny part of them.
The rest is hidden and protected by the skull.
Can you see where the eyes fit in this skull?

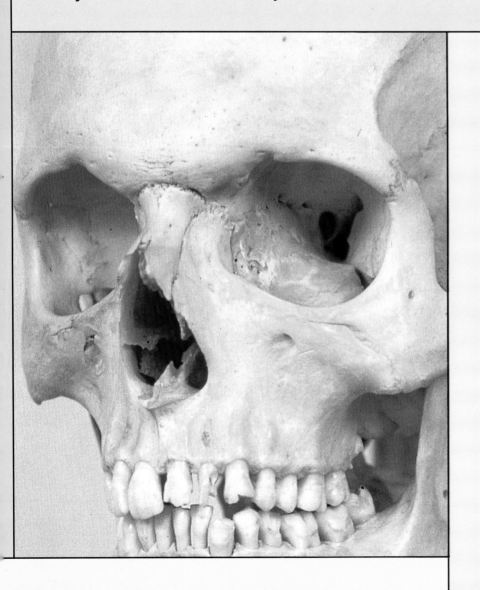

Eyes are protected in other ways.
Eyebrows stop sweat from running into them.
Sensitive eyelashes stop things
from brushing against your eye.

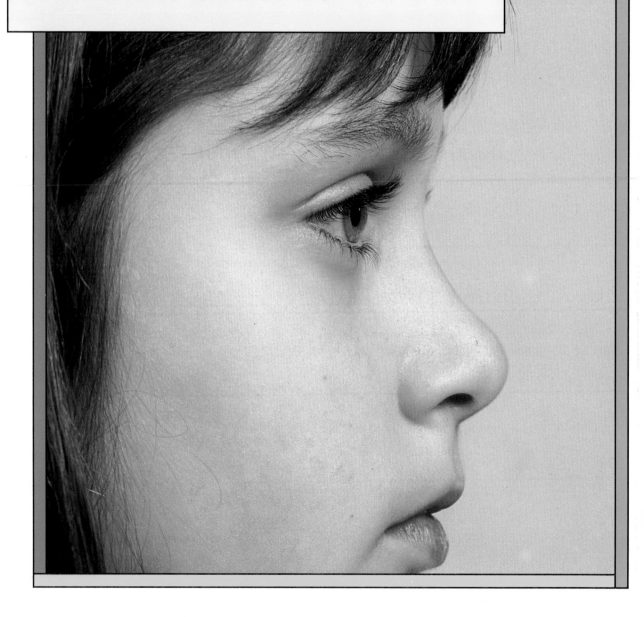

Eyelids are like windshield wipers.
Every time you blink, you wash salty tears
across the surface of your eyes.
This helps to keep them clean and moist.

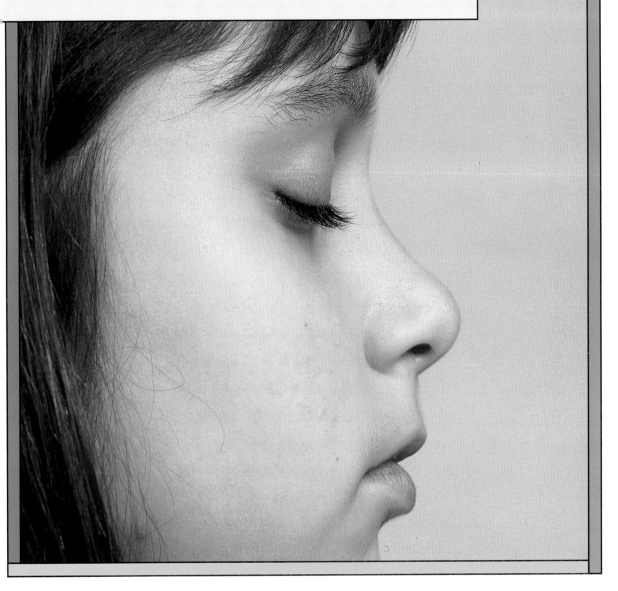

Sometimes eyes need extra protection –

under water,

on the road,

against the glare
of sun and snow

and against sparks
of fire and metal.

13

The colored ring in your eyes is called the iris.
The black hole in the middle of it is called the pupil.
It lets light through.

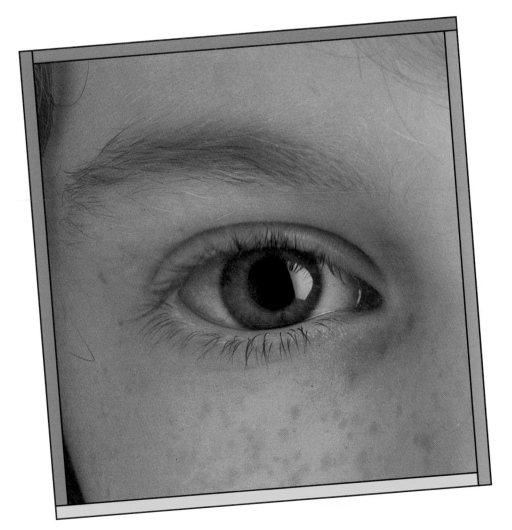

In dim light, the iris opens and the pupil widens
to let in as much light as possible.

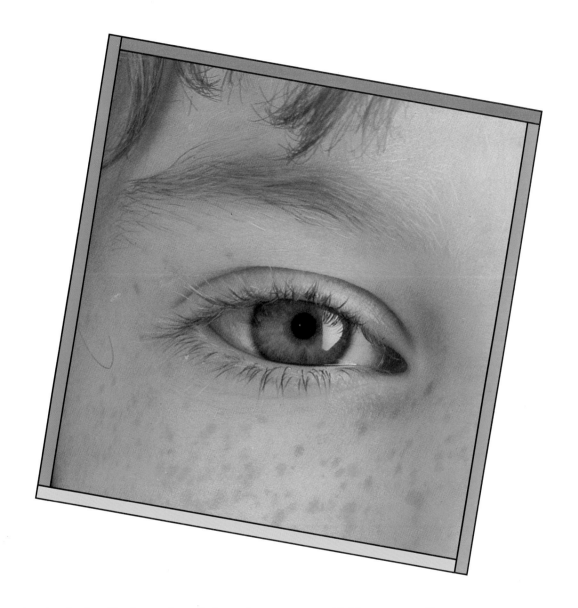

In bright light, the iris closes and the pupil narrows to stop too much light from getting in.

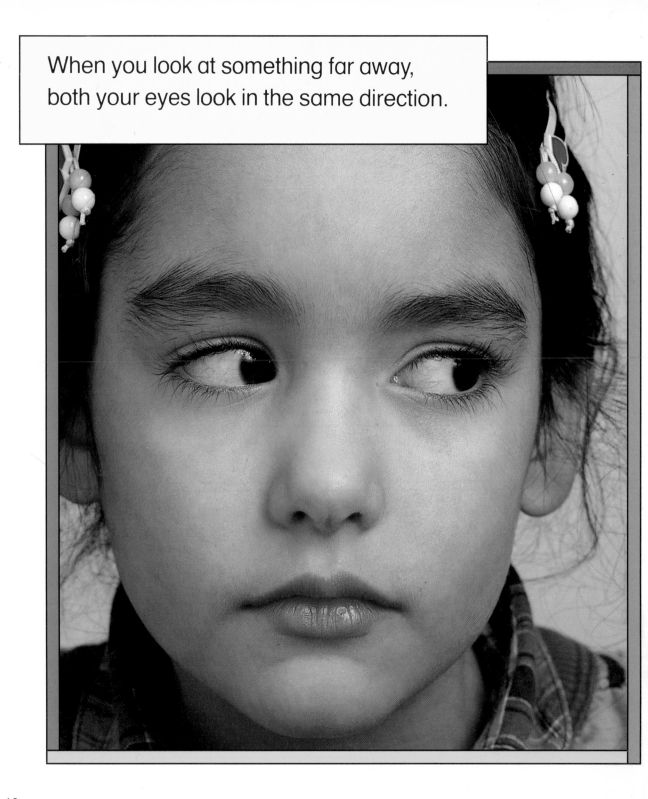

When you look at something far away,
both your eyes look in the same direction.

When you look at something very close, both eyes turn inward a little to see it more clearly.

17

Each eye sees a slightly different picture.
Hold out your thumb at arm's length.
Cover first one eye and then the other.
What do you notice?

This is what the left eye sees.   This is what the right eye sees.

Your brain puts the two pictures together
to form a complete scene.

Your eyes see things in color.

In dim light, you see only in shades of black, white and gray.

Some people do not see colors in the normal way.
Often they cannot tell red from green.
They are color-blind.

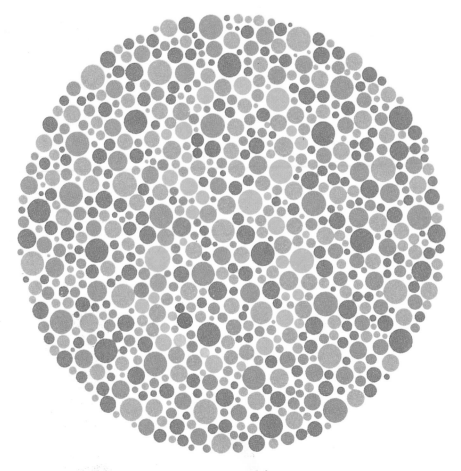

Look at this.
Can you see a number?
What is it?

Some people cannot see very clearly.
They wear glasses so that they can see better.

People who cannot see distant things clearly
are called near-sighted.
Their eyes can focus well only on close things.

People who cannot see close things very clearly
are called far-sighted.
Their eyes can focus well on things in the distance.

How do these instruments help us see things more clearly?

binoculars

telescope

monocle

magnifying glass

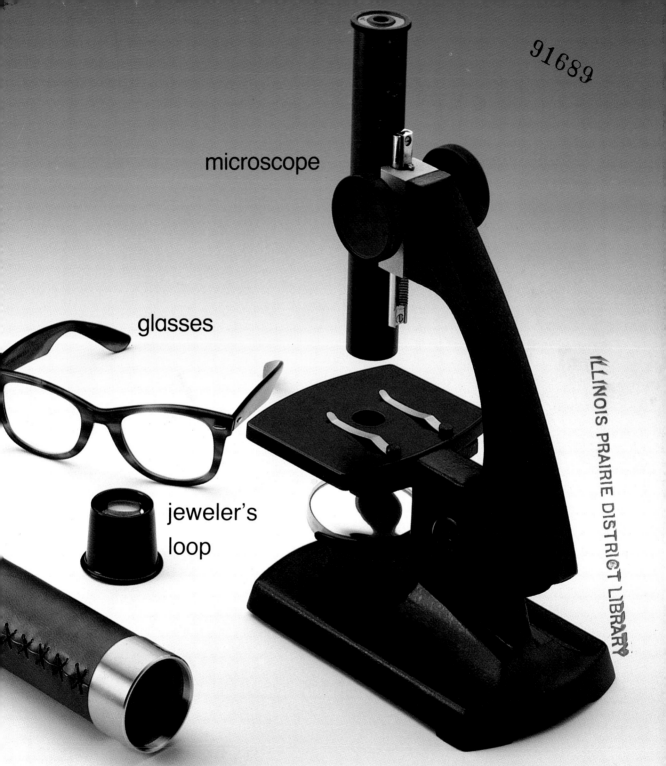

microscope

glasses

jeweler's
loop

91689

ILLINOIS PRAIRIE DISTRICT LIBRARY

What things might you look at with each instrument?

Some people cannot see at all.
They are blind.
What other senses do they depend upon
instead of sight?

Do you know?

● This is what your eye looks like inside.

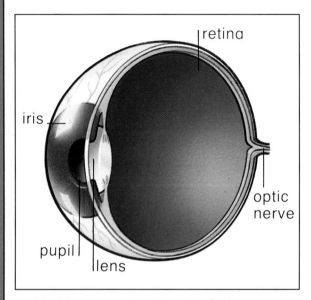

iris

retina

pupil

lens

optic nerve

Light enters the front of the eye through the pupil and passes through the lens.

The lens bends the light in such a way that a tiny picture of what you see is formed on the retina, the lining at the back of the eye. The picture is upside down and back to front.

Nerve fibers in the retina send a signal along the optic nerve to the brain.

The brain adjusts the picture so that it appears right side up again.

● Your eyeball is round and is the size of a ping pong ball. It is attached to six muscles that can roll the eye in any direction, so that you can see without continually moving your head.

● On the average, people blink 30 times a minute. You can't help blinking. It is automatic. If something is brought very close to your eyes, they shut at once to protect them from possible danger.

● It is impossible to keep your eyes open when you sneeze!

● The colored iris has tiny marks and patterns all over it. No two people's irises are identical.

● Blue eyes are more sensitive to light than brown ones. Brown eyes have more pigment (color) than blue ones.

Things to do

● Your eyes can trick you. Just because you think you see something does not mean that it is the way you think.

Fix your eyes on these squares. In a few moments, you will notice gray spots in the crosses made by the white lines. They are not really there at all. If you fix your gaze on one of the spots, it will disappear.

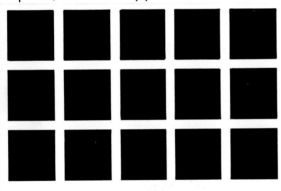

Judging distances is not always as easy as you think. Which line is longer: AB or CD?

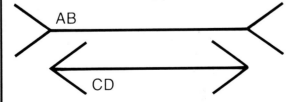

Check your answer with a ruler!

Sometimes things appear to change places while we look at them, even though they cannot move at all.

Look at this cheese. Does it look as if a slice has been cut out? Look again. Can you see a slice added on?

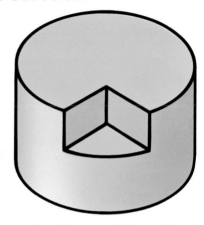

Keep looking at this table. At first you may see the top of it. Then things seem to change and you will think you are looking at the underneath.

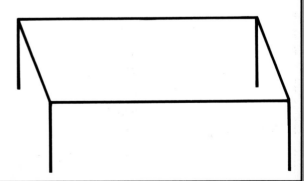

● Collect pictures and photographs of animals, birds and insects. Find out how their eyes compare with those of humans.

Look at where the eyes are placed. Are they on the front or the side of the head? Do they face forward or does the animal have all around vision? How big are the eyes in relation to the size of the head?

Do animals that are awake at night have different kinds of eyes from those that are awake during the day? What shape are their pupils?

Which animals rely on their eyes for finding food and which ones depend upon other senses? What difference do you notice about their eyes?

● The color of your eyes depends upon your parents. Do a survey among your friends to see which color eyes are the most common. Ask them what color their parents' eyes are as well. Make a note of the color of their hair and their skin and see if there is any relationhip between these and the color of their eyes.

Words about eyes

The word eye is used in many different ways. Can you find out what these words mean?

eyeful	eye-teeth
eye-catching	eye-witness
bull's eye	eye-bath
cat's eye	eye-shadow
eye-hole	eye-shot
eye-opener	eye-wash
eyesore	

Sayings about eyes

These are some sayings about eyes. What do you think they mean?

To cry one's eyes out
To turn a blind eye
To be up to the eyes
To see eye to eye
To keep an eye on
There's more than meets the eye
To keep one's eyes peeled
In the twinkling of an eye
A sight for sore eyes
One in the eye
To open someone's eyes

Index